Olive is an octopus.
She lives in the ocean.

Olive dreams of becoming a juggler.
She practices around the clock.

At one o'clock, Olive juggles an onion.

At two o'clock, Olive juggles an onion
and an old pair of overalls.

At three o'clock, Olive adds an owl
in an oak tree.

At four o'clock, Olive adds an orangutan.

At five o'clock, Olive adds an orange alien from outer space.

At six o'clock, Olive adds an entire orchestra.

At seven o'clock, Olive gets
oh so sleepy and...OOOPS!
Down come the onion
and the old pair of overalls

and the owl in the oak tree and the orangutan
and the orange alien from outer space
and even the entire orchestra—
right on Olive's head!

OUCH!

Now, Olive dreams of becoming an organist.
She practices around the clock.

How many things can you find that begin with the letter O?

See inside back cover for answers.

# Oo Cheer

O is for octopus who lives in the sea
O is for owl, high in a tree
O is for overalls and oars for a boat
O is for ostrich, orange, and oat
Hooray for O, big and small—
the most outstanding letter of all!